MW01289720

YOU
US
THEM

LinkedIn Marketing Concepts
for Nonprofit Professionals Who Really
Want to Make a Difference

Marc W. Halpert

ISBN 978-1719493833

Table of Contents

Introduction

Thank you, not only for buying this book, but for what you do.

And to set the record straight early, this is not a "how-to-do-this-or-that-on-LinkedIn" book. You are certainly not a "dummy."

This book, however, is designed to make you re-think your, and your organization's, role in the epic drama of making the world a better place and telling others about how to help you achieve it.

It's my goal to make you think of new ways to greatly improve that tired LinkedIn profile that reads like a résumé. I intend to make you just a bit uncomfortable, as it's hard, and for some unnerving, to reach higher to tell about yourself, in the context of the mission you work for.

Tell about yourself, in the context of the mission you work for.

I want you to shine. I want you to formulate your own words into phrases and ideas, so others will readily see how well you play your role, a subset of the organization you support and a vital one to articulate and draw others into your vision.

The challenge is that most of the people whom you aim to educate and impress might never speak to you, or meet you. Today, you are yet undiscovered by people who can help you and your mission, though they may be impressed with your vision. Many may revere you, but from afar, as they appreciate you for what good you do.

You work long hours, perhaps in unusual or challenging places, dealing with people and human issues that confront the conventions of our society, responsible for many more things at once than your corporate counterparts, ever increasingly challenged in what you want to accomplish.

You have accepted the unenviable task of asking others to part with their money and thus need to convince them that there will be good resulting from their decision, though they might not see a direct, tangible effect of their giving.

Often your compensation is more psychologically than financially enriching, because you firmly believe and take reward in the small steps to accomplish your view of a more orderly world, under ever-tightening budgetary constraints and erratic donation inflows.

You are a professional in one of the largest industries in the USA, perhaps the world, rubbing elbows with other good folks who strive for the same results for their respective mission, while competing for the same limited donor dollars. Yes, competing.

Your efforts are unique. Your vision is unique. Your tasks are unique. Your social media message must be unique too.

Your efforts are unique. Your vision is unique. Your tasks are unique. Your social media message must be unique too.

Yet so many nonprofit professionals mistakenly consider LinkedIn just a job board, when they could best be using LinkedIn as a competitive marketing tool, to relate personal stories that warm the hearts and open the wallets of the donor businesspeople on LinkedIn, who comprise a high-net-worth population you must continuously engage.

Yes, donors are businesspeople, too.

Within that elite donor business audience are talent pools of highly motivated and successful individuals: the prospective Board members you can recruit, the pro bono expert volunteers and potential professional staff whose skill sets you seek to utilize, the foundation administrators and grantors who now have an expedited way to evaluate you in their decision to give money to your cause, and the others you cannot readily see but who can be impressionably sympathetic to your cause. All are your LinkedIn marketing targets, now or at another time.

And they all think like consumers. It is essential to educate, enthrall, and market your organization's mission to them, since they may not yet have crossed the donation finish line. But you will not get them to move in your organization's direction, or carry them along further with your group in any meaningful way to obtain what you want from them, unless you impress on them the core need you serve and the message of what makes you unique, with access and exposure to your organization from top to bottom: from the most junior employee who has a face to the donor public, to the

Executive Director and the Board. Fundraising is a person-to-person process and seems to get more elaborate each year, with some momentary diversions, such as ice bucket challenges, that deviate from the tried-and-true. Thus, it's your challenge to take the usual storyline, and tell it again, ever more enticingly, continually.

Fundraising is a person-to-person process and seems to get more elaborate each year. Thus, it's your challenge to take the usual storyline, and tell it again, ever more enticingly, continually.

It's you, your organization, and your audience, with the welfare of the beneficiaries of your work in the balance, in a fresh and exciting face toward to the donor population.

It's You, Us, Them

The state of the art in social media is to act as a personal electronic touchpoint to the intended audience(s). And if you seek to attract the high-net-worth, accomplished, connected, and motivated subset of the business professional audience to supplement waning governmental and limited private grants and an ever-more competitive donation landscape, you need to step out and step it up, harnessing the power tool that LinkedIn is, when used effectively to reach new constituencies.

The concepts you will get from this book are deliberately tailored toward the people who work in and comprise nonprofits, NGOs, membership associations, etc. I will take you through the LinkedIn brand marketing ideas that really work in the nonprofit sector, which come from my past 17 years of experience marketing online donation and event registration services to nonprofit organizations.

Yes, amazing things can happen when you open yourself up and embrace LinkedIn as a technology power tool. But you must use it correctly to obtain maximum effect. Your adoption and interpretation of my pointers are convertible into your own way of expressing yourself, coordinating the message of your organization, and earning the respect and action of your existing and new followers:

Yes, amazing things can happen when you open yourself up and embrace LinkedIn as a technology power tool. But you must use it correctly to obtain maximum effect.

You, Us, Them.

That's where we are headed. And no better place to start than with "you." Then we'll fit "you" into "us" aligned as a part of your organization's brand and implore "them" to act and support your vision of a better world.

Each pronoun, you, us, them, is inclusive and embracing, especially when seen as part of the whole.

Colors and Shades

To ensure this book provides you the benefit it intends, please accept that there is an innate cohesion among the three sections:

- "You," one person, as a professional, the sum total of your past experience and present situations, always looking forward for yourself in your career, but looking to a better day for the mission and cause you so firmly believe in
- "Us," a team, an organization which can achieve amazing outcomes, small and large, when the combined talents and creativity are pooled and applied to the challenge at hand
- "Them," the aggregate of the people you seek as one-time and recurring stakeholders, for their time, expertise, money, influence and/or pro bono expert advice

It's the one, the few, and the many that overlap as we all commit to improving the world.

It's the one, the few, and the many that overlap as we all commit to improving the world.

No two individuals have the same way of expressing their commitment. Some cannot place it into words, but feel the need to help, but you as an individual need to say it your way, the organization needs to say it from a somewhat larger perspective, and the greater group must feel the passion, concern, and effort in doing great work to the point they are persuaded to assist.

Yes, there is bleeding (like watercolor or ink) from one section to the other, from one person to the group, from the group to the public. There is always the need to intentionally channel the data and emotion; it's never succinct. There are always shades of meaning in what you say or show. Each tint melds with the one next to it to create a new hue. Eventually as you stand back, it all comes together, like an Impressionist painting.

So, open your mind to the rainbow of tangible opportunity when you use words, graphics, and gestures to market your brand to a ready and willing business professional social network.

Enter with old mores and practices left behind. What I am about to expose you to is by no means comprehensive.

So, open your mind to the rainbow of tangible opportunity when you use words, graphics, and gestures to market your brand to a ready and willing business professional social network. Enter with old mores and practices left behind.

Rather, the next pages are designed to sensitize you to opportunities you will want to convert to your personality and viewpoint.

You

One single professional
who makes a big difference

Prologue

You are a selfless individual, working diligently to achieve a better world, with opinions, skills, ethics, and experience unique to your career history.

Perhaps you were raised by parents, educators, or religious leaders to make a difference. Some claim helping others is hardcoded into their DNA. Many are "bitten" by the bug by some experience in their past to bring about their lifelong commitment to helping others.

Today, professionals are encouraged by their companies to give back to their community, further using their skill set and building effective teams more readily. Some people find themselves volunteering, then morphing into the management of the organization, as the natural outgrowth of the expertise they originally donated. And it's increasingly evident to me, from nonprofit pros I meet, that many have spent the bulk of their professional time in a corporate environment, and later decided to migrate to the nonprofit sector in an encore career.

Regardless, no two nonprofit pros are alike. Let's show the professional world just that.

Regardless, no two nonprofit pros are alike. Let's show the professional world just that.

Tell Your Story, Stand Apart

As you moved along in the nonprofit industry, you grew new layers in your experience, based on your expertise, vision, and passion. I meet people like you all the time in my work, and many tell me they want their profile to be better representative of them on LinkedIn, but hesitate to express what makes them and their organization's mission, as an extension of them, special.

Or fund-worthy.

I find among nonprofit pros, in various generations (no matter which one you hail from), that they consider LinkedIn to be some sort of amorphous cloud, meant for "suits" only. Or worse, they see it as an unpalatable necessity, only of utility when a job change is involved, as if it were some sort of online job board, used then discarded.

Do you say that to yourself? Did I hit a common thread of (mis)conception?

LinkedIn is so much more than that. Only if you tell your story to the reader. And no one can tell your story as well as you can, or should.

You Plus More

I often equate LinkedIn to a power tool in your self-marketing toolbox. But you cannot drive a nail with a power screwdriver. You need to learn how to effectively use LinkedIn as a branding mechanism that will place you in the nonprofit marketplace to achieve anything you desire, or dream of.

I often equate LinkedIn to a power tool in your self-marketing toolbox.

I often remark that great business-people all seem to know each other and are networked in the most astonishing ways. And the same is true in the microcosm of nonprofit players. There are many overlapping small networks that make up the larger ones we participate in.

Interconnectivity abounds, about four degrees separating us one from the other, although I think it is closer now to two-point-something to three. Several years ago, a study found it to be four:

> https://well.blogs.
> nytimes.com/2011/11/22/
> four-degrees-of-separation

Certainly, it's fewer than four in today's social media era given the ensuing six years' social media evolution, and then further, within the close-knit nonprofit world.

So far, it's all about you. But it's much more than you and whom you know. The rest of your peers in the nonprofit sector want to get to know you, and you them. *It's a two-way street to network, and as you well know, it's better to give than receive.*

Let's look at you in a different way.

Take a Competitive Survey

I always say everyone is amazing, but most just cannot completely, effectively tell just why and how they are *amazing-er* (as I call it) than their competitor (no matter how they define the competition). But how do you best differentiate yourself and self-define to make an impression? How do you beat the competition? Figure out who or what the competition is, to start.

I hope you will acknowledge that you compete for:

- the same donor attention and their dollars, as does another professional like you in another organization, marketing their need and mission as every bit as important as yours, if not more

- airtime, with clarity of purpose and message and immediacy of the problem you seek to remedy to educate the public
- space and position on the right social media platforms that command attention from your target audience
- coverage and referral by influencers you cultivate, for their reach and the downstream impressions they make on others
- the very short bandwidth of attention we all suffer from these days, and by extension for donors' absorption of your message into their memory
- employment applications from new staffers with revolving-door careers, to draw them to a vacant position; a delay in filling can stymie a project or disrupt an office, and never comes at a good time
- consideration by prospective employees: development pros and/or officers with the right set of skills and experience (and rolodexes of donors!)
- the compensation and benefits package that will retain staffers who have not yet left you
- time and consultation from volunteers or pro bono experts who personally identi-

fy with your work, commit the time, and must feel appreciated

- the time, expertise, and commitment of Board members who before joining your Board evaluated and identified with your message on social media, LinkedIn included (especially the business users of LinkedIn, experienced in using it well)

- funders and grant makers who will eventually and increasingly use LinkedIn as another input into their competitive decision making, assessing your worthiness for their awards

- match funding from corporate employees' personal donations with those from their company

- competitive funding from corporate and private foundations who deem your presence and mission in line with their community-minded purposes

Those are just a *few* ways you compete, in no particular order!

Whenever I discuss the competitive landscape with nonprofit pros, their eyes dart as I outline just some of the above bullets with them. They don't always grasp that it's a competitive marketplace, until I refocus them.

Meanwhile, your competitors are striving to extract the best marketing message and funding from each communication medium, LinkedIn included. That's why this LinkedIn book is necessary to your personal use, your organization's brand, and especially your stakeholders' perceptions.

Nonprofit pros must take proactive and aggressive branding actions in concerted, intelligent ways.

You must excel. You knew that. I will amend what I just stated: more importantly, you must convey **why** and **how** you excel. And that's hard to do for many. Nearly impossible for some. Needed by all.

You must convey why and how you excel.

My job: to show you the benefits, making this less painful. Notice I never said it would be easy or fast. It's a process, just like the one that got you to where you are today.

Morphing Through Experiences

Your career as a nonprofit professional comes from a mashup of experiences, planned and unplanned. In past decades, I doubt many people studied in college or graduate school to become a nonprofit pro. Rather, a series of life events brought you to your current position.

16

I recall conversations with colleagues who are Directors of Development or Executive Directors: in retracing their careers, they did not start out with their executive position as an imagined endpoint. Often, they were corporate executives who learned business through a for-profit lens. They were elevated to new roles and learned in those positions to evaluate business opportunities for optimal profitability. Perhaps this resonates with your history.

Then something happened to you.

Perhaps as a millennial or other young professional, you see nonprofit service as the first step in a budding career path serving others. No matter what you majored in, where you went to school, when you graduated, or where you ranked in your class, nonprofit work wooed you. Not because it's trendy or others are doing it, but because it's your deep passion.

It may have been a promotion; it may have been a layoff. Or a protracted absence from business due to family obligations, or a transfer to a rotation in the company foundation: these events sealed your fate in some way(s) as a giver. Layer on top the expanding desire to volunteer your time and expertise and offer your fresh viewpoints to help guide an organization.

The switch to the nonprofit sector turned your valuable prior training around: from a focus on monetary goals to humanitarian reward. Your ROI men-

The switch to the nonprofit sector turned your valuable prior training around: from a focus on monetary goals to humanitarian reward.

tality shifted to return-to-the-community. In turn, you gave up a rosy career trajectory and its monetary reward as your altruism widened.

As I like to say, no one can ever take your experience away. Rather, it awaits your triggering it, since you add layers as you progress, then implement based on what you know, thus improving every event or project you engage in. You merely pull that experience card from your back pocket as needed, often dusty and perhaps not used in decades. It's just in deep freeze and then defrosted for the current task at hand. Only you have access to it, at will. Your mind races with electricity to bring these memories forward to be used again today.

Using this wealth of experience, you move up from organization to organization, from one subject area to another that demands ever more monetary and active attention for the sake of the world as you see it. Your job is to articulate your caring, to enable others to care as much as you do. You must compel others to think as you do and then act along with you.

It's a marketing job, at the end of the day: why you, aside from others?

It's a marketing job, at the end of the day: *why you*, aside from others?

The prospect of saving just one more life, or improving one more animal's welfare, or using another scientific improvement to preserve the fragile environment, or bringing clean water to an indigenous tribe for the first time in its history: these make the heart swell and beat a bit faster, in a good way!

But how do you express this rich, compelling, experiential narrative on LinkedIn, especially if parents and teachers admonished you not to talk about yourself?

Articulate Exactly What Makes You YOU

In an attention-deprived, consumer-action world, you get very few nanoseconds to describe your role, passion, and mission. You need to use powerful, picturesque words and phrases, graphical illustrations, and video to fix your impact in the reader's memory. It's the combination of experiences that makes you stand apart from others' equally compelling demands.

The reinforcement of why <u>your</u> message is best must be concise, colorful, clear, and coordinated. *Then you are memorable*. Proponents of any cause must overcome skepticism and cynicism and show the worth of their vision. Words can express it. Graphics can add color to it. Videos add color, plus action, plus sound. Stir them together for your message. Then you are compelling, actionable.

Let's focus on improving each section of your LinkedIn personal profile. How do you start?

Look at your existing LinkedIn profile. Each day, at the time of day you are freshest, most creative, and undistracted, start to re-write a single section of your LinkedIn profile a few (five or six) times with your word-processing software, each new time on a blank screen independently of the previous try. Save them separately, and then copy-paste all half-dozen drafts to a single page and yellow-highlight the best of each attempt. Then "shuffle the cards" to meld together the highlighted best from each into a master version of the "best of the best." Massage it some more until it shines. Later, perhaps on other days, repeat the same process to craft the next successive LinkedIn section on your profile.

Now you have something that begins to tell your story in each section, in crisp words and colorful phrases, and assuming you are honest and conscientious in these exercises, you have a great brand story coming together, the story of you: your self-perception, your career, your skill set, woven into the fabric of your value proposition.

Don't rush or cheat this creative process. It will come together for you, with time and effort.

Refine it to the point when you can show it to an objective colleague (or a few of them) whose opinion(s) you respect, and ask for an honest critique. Ask each: does it adequately tell what my worth is to the market, from the outside reader's point-of-view?

Accept their honesty and coopt their changes into your draft profile.

Then step back and read it aloud to yourself. Make sure it flows well. Look for flaws in parallel format, voice, tone, tenses, typos, and once perfect, congratulate yourself: surely it breaks new ground in your self-branding.

But _only you_ can make it more compelling and indicative of the value you bring to the market. Keep on tweaking your own words, as needed. You will find the need to improve your profile constantly.

Earlier, we established how you need to self-express and differentiate. Take a hard look at each rewritten section in your profile to be sure it resonates with the power of you, confidently addressing why and how you can help someone

> _But only you can make it more compelling and indicative of the value you bring to the market. Keep on tweaking your own words, as needed._

or some organization. Use full sentences, persuasive narrative, and reinforced points to make a great personal LinkedIn profile.

You already are amazing (see my comments above), but you need to convince the casual LinkedIn reader just how amazing you are. That's you brand-marketing yourself. Your goal: look "amazing-er" as I like to say, always improving on your earlier profile and certainly staying ahead of the competition! No better place to show it than LinkedIn!

Advisory: the following pointers will help you organize the rote actions of making your profile more complete (section by section). Do not stop midstream, as many people do and erroneously use elementary ideas to fill in the blanks with *who* and *what*. Challenge yourself with the quality of the more introspective concept of *why* you do what you do. Don't cheat yourself.

This "why" concept and its bearing on the sections of the LinkedIn personal profile is covered in depth in my book *LinkedIn Marketing Techniques for Law and Professional Practices* published by the American Bar Association in June 2017, available on Amazon or Barnes & Noble, or of course, The ABA, at shopaba.org.

There are 168 pages of ideas in that book that will apply to you, as a professional, *the title of the book notwithstanding*, (OK, one chapter concerns ethical considerations for attorneys, so you have my permission to skip that! But read the rest if you wish to gain the full experience). The book draws on the concepts in Simon

Sinek's *Start with Why*, which I encourage you to read and to adopt its wisdom.

Let's take the LinkedIn profile apart, section by section, and briefly analyze opportunities for you to better brand yourself as a nonprofit professional, from the top.

Make Your Brand Attractive

Cola, in essence, is just a brown, wet, fizzy, and sweet liquid, but the expenditure of hundreds of millions of dollars a year on marketing and branding repeatedly draws our preferred taste towards one cola brand over another, as a repeat consumer. Competition for your cerebral attention, memory, and increased sensory attraction go hand-in-hand with branding.

You should be recognizable as a brand, too.

Starting at the top of your LinkedIn personal profile page:

- Use a background banner at the top showing you in action or engaged in the cause, with you principally in the foreground. Again, remember, it's about the reader better visualizing *you*.

- Add a crisp and professional headshot photo. Just your face, shoulders to top of head (unless you are an animal rights advocate, then you and your pet and other preferred species are fine, as long as we can easily see your face in the photo). Your face is your visual recognition to acquaint others.

- Use graphic art in the Summary and/or Experience sections, topically appropriate to the section, and be sure you show an array of various media that you are comfortable in: slide decks, videos, podcasts, PDFs, white papers, etc. They add depth and color to create allure to the brand of you. Describe each item briefly in carefully-selected words, so the reader knows what he/she is about to open. Periodically, it's a good idea to double check that the links still work.

- Associate the logos of the organization you work/worked for with the Experience section for added visual recognition of the time you spent there. Again, this provides color and interest, especially when a brand of the organization is instantly recognizable and impressive. That brand adds to your reputation.

- Make your narrative interesting and conversational in each LinkedIn section, as if you are speaking in a business-like manner to the reader. Use power verbs (Google "185 power verbs" to find a great list), and avoid weak ones like "was" and "had" and "made," since you are speaking about yourself here, marketing your wealth of education, experience, and vision, not just chatting.

- Use short paragraphs. Employ bullets sparingly. This is not a memo. It must be interesting, so allow the reader to appreciate the depth of your experience. Make it visually interesting too, in words, phrases, and pictures that illustrate your points.

Most importantly, do not make it another résumé or CV. These are never as interesting to read, with their look backward, bland voice, and prescribed format, limited to two pages, black-and-white, as if engraved in stone. Your résumé won't suffice to tell your story, so do not get complacent about the reader figuring out how well suited you are to the goal. You need to step forward as a brand and make your LinkedIn per-

Do not make your profile another résumé or CV. These are never as interesting to read, with their look backward, bland voice, and prescribed format, limited to two pages, black-and-white, as if engraved in stone.

sonal profile organic, that is, it changes with you, it profiles you personally to impress someone, updated with your most current viewpoints and your unique voice, coming right through to the reader, reflecting your latest and greatest narrative.

Do you think this is easy? It's not. I have found that those with a shortcut mentality rarely do a good job of portraying themselves as successful professionals. What I do see in my practice as a LinkedIn coach: it's a matter of individuals being in touch with their credentials, able to articulate the value proposition they bring to the proverbial table. Then the LinkedIn profile soars.

It can be measured by one's ability to add color and relevance to an electronic screen and light it up with great stories of a career journey that is not nearly over yet. Crafting the right words and images is the goal, as you think about your branding: your physical, emotional, and mental imaging. A casual reader needs more than facts to become entranced with your story and message.

It takes each reader a different amount of time and varying number of touchpoints to digest your information. No one will reach deep into their pocket after you put forth one fact or express one emotional appeal.

I want to finish this discussion with the advisory that it takes each reader a different amount of time and varying number of touchpoints to digest your information. No one will reach deep into their pocket after you put forth one fact or express one emotional appeal. Feel free to be repetitious throughout your profile; just re-inforce the central concept in different ways, germane to the profile section you place it in.

Be Searchable;
Four Sections in Particular

LinkedIn as of now is composed of over 550 million business professionals, and many use it daily as their database, their rolodex, their connectivity to the world they nurture. For those of us who see it as a continuous branding mechanism, it can be used continually to market ourselves to the believers or to those we want to influence. Be findable in their search. Use it wisely and frequently, and it can reward you.

First recognize that databases in the online environment are search-term sensitive, so on your personal LinkedIn profile in four very important places, decide which search terms people would use to find you in this database. You may want to ask your website developer what metatags and key words were included for search engine optimization and use these words in the following vitally important, searchable sections of your personal LinkedIn profile:

- **Headline** (the 120-character teaser just under your name) tells in a quick nibble why you do what you do and where your values and passions are; certainly not a bland title like "Director of Development at XYZ.org," but rather a more introspective, informative "Experienced Development Director enacting creative methods to encourage donors to actually enjoy their giving experience." That's exactly 120 characters, including spaces. You should get creative with your headline. It should make readers want to know more, so they will read downward into your profile for additional material, next covered in the Summary.

- **Summary** is, in effect, a further explanation of the Headline, with much more room to go into detail, as if this were your elevator pitch: pithy, smart, and enticing. Tell why you, what you are known for, with a call to action to give you the opportunity to show how truly amazing you are. Here you can go into more detail in preparation for the Experience section, especially about your current position and about how past positions layer into your professional expertise today.

- Each segment of your **Experience** section chronicles the successes and challenges you rose to in various jobs in your past. This is what makes you who you are today, with accomplishments explained to resonate and show your rich background and wins. Be mindful: this is not a place to talk about the organization you work/worked for. This is about <u>you</u> individually, and what <u>you</u> achieved.

- **Skills** are self-defined descriptors that demonstrate talents you possess from past experience and that you use today and bring with you everywhere you go: now and in the future. Be exact in your listed skills. For example, "Nonprofits" is not a skill, but "Nonprofit Merger Integration" is. Endorsements from colleagues add to the interest factor in your specific skill. And be sure that endorsers truly know you for that skill, otherwise remove their endorsement. Be honest and complete, but do not be too broad or boastful.

Using keywords throughout these four sections optimizes the LinkedIn search engine to capture them, and thus you, making you part of a short list of people the searcher can consider. It's your story with its past-present-future orientation encouraging them to spend time, progressing through your story from the top headline teaser to the elevator pitch to more details about your job experience. And beyond that too!

Using keywords throughout these four sections optimizes the LinkedIn search engine to capture them, and thus you, making you part of a short list of people the searcher can consider.

Notice that a well-constructed profile enables a casual reader to absorb as much about you in a short reading as they can and encourages the reader to peruse as far down your LinkedIn profile page as you can get them to read.

That means you must preplan your profile, sketch it out, and be ready to go through an editing process as I earlier suggested. It is not easy. It takes time, thought, and effort.

And that said, I am providing my LinkedIn concepts here at a very high level. Each time I work directly with a professional, we break down one section at a time for the best branding techniques and marketing practices in each, all customized to the client's specific needs. No two clients are ever alike! If you desire more personalized guidance, please inquire about my one-to-one global coaching.

Keep in mind that so far we are speaking only about you here, not about your organization. There's lots of room for the organization to have its own company profile page on LinkedIn. Your personal profile is your personal chance to shine on your own.

I presume you seek a better world and more opportunity for yourself as well, as you progress, because there's a big revolving door of nonprofit jobs out there and you can move up and out if you want. But no one will speak to you or see you unless they perceive you as a worthy candidate. Who else can tell better about yourself than you? That's just the point: be yourself, but be your marketing, branding self and elaborate these colorful points on LinkedIn.

Keep in mind that so far we are speaking only about you here, not your organization. There's lots of room for the organization to have its own company profile page on LinkedIn.

Speak About Yourself as "I"

Keep readers enthralled as if you are speaking to them personally. Present your career orientation with the pronoun "I" as you make the case *why you,* and why the crowd you surround yourself with will want to refer you. Don't be stingy with the narrative, thinking people either do not care or will consider you ego-centric. Never refer to your-

Present your career orientation with the pronoun "I" as you make the case why you, and why the crowd you surround yourself with, will want to refer you.

self as "he" or "she," or worse, "Mr./Ms. (last name)." Who talks like that?

There is a very rich story to tell of your multiyear career that makes you an ideal candidate for various business opportunities; put it in your own vocabulary and perspective, overcome the fear of talking about yourself, and find that delicate balance of enough narrative vs. overblown, verbose TMI (too much information). You know the limit of most readers' attention spans. Make the most of it.

Use the electronic real estate LinkedIn provides you to put forth your story well. Create the fabric of *why you* as a collection of colorful and well-woven threads.

Did You Take a Career Hiatus?

Repeating my previous concepts on how marketing yourself is very different than setting out bald, re-sume-y factoids, I encourage you to make the most out of seemingly disparate aspects of your history: tell why events and decisions in your career happened the way they did.

Not covering them means the reader must make assumptions, which are often incorrect and lead to a distorted view. Or the reader gets frustrated in his/ her short attention span and leaves you behind as a discredited prospect, never to return and give you a second chance. So, tell us the reason and the cause/ effect of actions you took to bridge any career or skill gaps. Honestly narrate that part of your career story.

Perhaps you took time off for:

- a career path or industry change (as seems common in the nonprofit sector)
- a period of long-term unemployment due to a recession or another reason
- at-home obligations such as raising children, caring for a sick relative
- a part-time position to ease into your new role
- a temp-to-hire period to adjust to a changing work environment

LinkedIn provides a good slide deck to help you work out the best way to address a career break. Have a look at LinkedIn's appropriate suggestions, especially surrounding what best to say in your headline:

https://blog.linkedin.com/2014/04/17/ how-to-represent-your-unique-career-path- on-your-linkedin-profile-slideshare

The rest of your profile must reflect the same theme as your headline, of course.

More Sections to Tell *Why You*

Let's examine in more depth a few other sections in the personal LinkedIn profile. (*Don't forget to pay extra attention to those four search-word sensitive sections: Headline, Summary, Experience, and Skills that we already touched on. These comments expand on my earlier ones to better tell why you*).

Some of the following sections are not well used, if used at all. Optimize them, along with the other four, to improve your imagery and story:

- **Background photo:** Found at the very top of your LinkedIn personal profile page, attach a great wide-view picture (or stitch a few into a mosaic) showing you in action. If it's you with the kids from the African village school you built and support, or you working to engineer the water and sanitation hygiene of an indigenous Central American tribe, or you display a panorama of a packed gala raising money for the mission, or…or… then you can make a strong and memorable visual digital impression in 1584 (w) x 396 (h) pixels. Choose carefully. Change as needed—it's easy and fast.

- **Headshot:** It's small and round on your LinkedIn profile, but it can be expanded to see better when clicked, your photo should be your face front and center. It must be easy to memorize so readers can recall what you look like when they eventually meet you. Please be honest with yourself -- replace those old photos that no longer look like you. Make sure yours is in color, high resolution, and preferably professionally taken. Dress business casual or more formal if you think it matters to your audience. A natural background behind you is better than a gray fake-stormy backdrop like we all had in grade school. This is not the place for the organization's logo, please.

- **Contact Information:** Please make it easy for potential employers, donors, or other stakeholders to contact you in any method they prefer; this may not be the one you are most used to, or you prefer. Provide your email and mailing/street addresses. You can only show one phone number (increasingly you should start using your mobile number so you can receive text messages). You can show multiple website addresses: a URL for your organization, a blog URL if applicable, a personal website URL, a Twitter handle (yours or your organization's) and finally please take the time to personalize your LinkedIn URL. To accomplish this very easy task that far too many people ignore, see

https://www.linkedin.com/help/linkedin/answers/personal%20url

- **Graphics:** Include some that accentuate any narrative in your Summary or your Experience sections. Remember, a picture is worth a thousand words and a video can be worth multiples of that. Use images judiciously to prove your point in a memorable way.

  Demonstrate you are adept at capably writing, speaking, and presenting. The lack of these skills is lamented by employers and recruiters as a failure of the higher education system and a direct result of our online electronic message society, so include a recent piece or two. Include examples of diverse writing styles and levels of complexity, making sure it is material you have the legal right to show. If you are in doubt, either ask permission or find something else.

Other graphic formats to consider with some comments about each:

- **Documents and presentations:** (.pdf, .ppt, .pps, .pptx, .ppsx, .pot, .potx, .odp. .doc, docx, .rtf, .odt): Since any type of graphic can be converted to a PDF, choose documents or picture presentations that demonstrate your ability to compose, present, and convince others. I'll offer the same advisory on PDFs or slide decks: nothing sensitive or private should be shown that your organization does not want made public; again, ask for permission if you have any concerns. If you are not the sole author of the material, cite the co-author(s). Include articles, white papers, email blasts, direct mail fundraising material, annual reports, etc. Provide the URL if the material appeared online and a brief description of what the reader is about to open for context (topic, where shown, why it was created, to whom it was presented, date, success of the appeal, etc.), so you are not perceived as possibly wasting the reader's time.

- **Images:** (.png, .jpg, .jpeg, .bmp, .gif, .tiff): Use photos of events, news coverage, galas, and any other events or activities that tell the reader that you stand apart.

- **Audio and video files:** (audio: .aac, .mp3, and Vorbis; video: .asf, .avi, .flv, .mpeg-1, .mpeg-4, .mkv, QuickTime, WebM, H264/AVC, .mp4, .vp8, .vp9, .wmv2, and .wmv3). Use them wisely — not too lengthy or too frequently. Identify what the viewer is about to see and hear. These formats can be quite powerful in ramming a theme home by placing them directly and appropriately in your Summary or Experience sections. I suggest you carefully select the thumbnail graphic associated with the audio or video file so in one glance readers can decide whether to open it. Audio or video files that run too long in duration will make the reader drift off, or away, from your profile, so none longer than one minute; less if possible. Or provide the reader a time stamp within the description of the file so they can skip to that place in the audio or video for quicker access.

- **Education:** Show all secondary education, even if you did not complete a college or graduate degree. And please do not be afraid of revealing the years you attended, as the reader probably already has a good idea of your age based on your career history. LinkedIn also offers alumni pages, so your university classmates can find you and you them, making it ideal for you to approach fellow alums for help in your mission. It's up to you whether you want to include your high school years. You should consider adding work-study or study abroad, both well-rounding experiences. If you wrote a thesis or dissertation pertinent to your field of work now, include the URL so interested readers can open it and read a brief abstract. This is not the place to be overly technical; please save that for the document itself.

- **Volunteer Experience:** This is the place to show your out-of-the-office volunteer work, pro bono advisor activity, mentorships, Board memberships, etc. Briefly explain your work in terms of the expertise and skill set(s) you provide as a volunteer. Think "marketing" in your narrative: not "stuffing envelopes for a fundraiser;" but rather "managing a paper-based contact campaign for lapsed donors to reinvigorate their giving." You are merely showing your skill set in the best possible light, as you offer it to an organization needing your expertise. Again, it's part of self-marketing.

Only YOU Can Shortchange
Your Accomplishments

Elaborate in the various Accomplishments subsections in your LinkedIn profile those achievements you earned: honors, awards, certifications, publications, patents, language fluency, and courses. I find highly successful professionals are ironically reticent to tell about these milestones, which are especially impressive when nominated or awarded by peers for great work. Modesty has its place; not here. It's not bragging; rather, it's showing your accomplishments in terms of *why you*: why you were chosen, why you earned it, why your point of view was recognized from among many who contributed, etc.

Do not just lay out the facts; rather, describe the branding and the backstory behind each Accomplishment entry on your LinkedIn profile.

Do not just lay out the facts; rather, describe the branding and the backstory behind each Accomplishment entry on your LinkedIn profile, and do not hesitate to share the latest news, as new accomplishments ensue, immediately. Posting the achievement as an update on your LinkedIn home page to connections is great, but short-lived like a snowflake in a snowstorm buried among the thousands that follow it. Simultaneously to posting to your home page, update the same news to the appropriate subsection of Accomplishments on your personal profile to memorialize a career event.

Have you changed industries? Don't forget that achievements in a former industry can usually apply in your new industry. It's the same you. I recommend that you adapt the details of an achievement in the former industry to the readers in the new industry, again using marketing-speak. Since you earned it, show it, but adapt it to a new reading population's perception.

Regardless of your past background, present orientation, and future direction, you are the best one to tell your own story. When crafted well, different aspects of your experience weave together in a career journey with your rich, diverse experience, skills, and accomplishments.

Now a few more concepts about specific Accomplishment subsections:

- **Honors and Awards:** If peers awarded you or recognized you, that's impressive, especially among your other peers. Do not assume we know what the award is about, its awarding body, or why this is important to you and to others. Explain the honor, and what you did to deserve it. Go a bit deeper here when explaining, mindful it's the quality of what you say that makes a more lasting impression as the honoree, and by whom it is bestowed. Include a URL to the press release and/or organization itself that awarded the honor, so the reader can explore that organization's mission, too.

- **Certifications:** This is another section to show some exceptional achievement, where academics meld with experience, even if in a different subject area. Those letters after your name can often transfer to other fields, but you must tell us how you earned them. If the certification or license must be renewed, show us the term and expiration date of the current one you possess. If you have let a credential lapse, think about whether it would be useful to include it — even lapsed CPAs know a lot about finance.

- **Courses:** If you attended any courses outside a degree program, mention them here. Perhaps it's an advanced course in financial statement analysis for nonprofit professionals. That's a differentiator vs. someone without that same training. Articulate how you use this course knowledge in your work. Be deliberate in explaining why the investment in your education is worthwhile for you and your organization, in terms of augmenting your regular work to enhance your career. Tell us. It's part of your skill set now.

If you are an adjunct professor, what are you teaching? At what levels and where? Are you an instructor in an alternative educational environment or online? In any of these situations, with a little finagling of the Courses subsection, you can show the reader you are an expert in your field, so much so that you impart your experience and wisdom to others in a classroom setting. Tell us how you have found teaching rewarding.

- **Publications:** Repeating myself, but this is important: we want to know how well you write. When you are published, tell us. Have you authored a white paper that you distributed to others in your field? Give a short summary of what the article was about. Note: don't be bashful here either; even if you are quoted and didn't write the article, this is meaning-ful, showing you as a source to the press. Put context around that article: where published (not everyone is familiar with the publication, so provide the impor-tance of its being published there), why the article was timely, cite attribution to your co-author, if appropriate, when it appeared, and its intent and success. Ask readers to freely share your article with their networks — make it go viral. And finally, curate great articles your connec-tions write and share them, a lot.

- **Languages:** Do you speak a foreign lan-guage as part of your daily work in your NGO, for example? Self-determine your proficiency from LinkedIn's prescribed levels. Be honest. And as a segué, did you know you can translate your LinkedIn profile into another language? See

https://www.linkedin.com/help/linkedin/answer/1717?query=translate%20profile

- **Projects:** Give us an update on a major long-term project you are engaged in. I showed in my LinkedIn profile my writ-ing this book as a project, to keep my con-nections apprised of my ongoing activity

> and demonstrate leadership in my field.
> Include in-work projects too, so long as
> you let us know what strategic tasks you
> are completing, why they're important,
> who they are aimed at, and when you
> expect completion.

The bottom line: assumptions readers must make for lack of adequate information are usually not as accurate or positive (and certainly you know better than we), so set the record straight about why this is part of your branding. Success is not awarded to shy people, so why be one on LinkedIn?

You and Your Connected World

Here is where we begin to diverge a bit: not just about you, your efforts, and the reasons *why* you do them, but now we pivot to others on whom you rely and who depend on you, in return:

> • **Recommendations** from/to trusted and
> appreciated cheerleaders: ask for and
> give accolades in narrative form. Those
> valuable people stick with you as either
> recommender or recommended, from/to

LinkedIn connections, from those who have witnessed your prowess first hand or whom you have been dramatically impressed. These are not simple one-click endorsements of your skills or their skills, by contrast.

- Ask for recommendations. When you get an email or phone call commending you for a project especially well done, ask the other person (this presumes you are connected to them on LinkedIn) to commit those words to a written LinkedIn recommendation, to appear prominently on your personal profile. Otherwise, the momentary great feeling will fade and is lost forever.

- Never use the boiler-plate recommendation request language; if you do, you will receive a lame recommendation in nearly every instance. Rather, manage this process by drafting the barebones of what you want them to say in your recommendation requests: because you guide the writer, each new recommendation can be managed to cover a different aspect of your skills and accomplishments. Also suggest they append an anecdote of your yeoman work (you may need to remind them). They will appreciate your helping make this exercise more efficient for them, and you are more likely to receive the type of recommendation you were looking for. Then recognize you do not have to publish a recommendation that contains an error, typo, or misspelling of your name, or if it is not as good as you expected; just return it to the writer and point out the changes you would like made. They should be happy to do this for you.

- Give recommendations to those who deserve it, without their asking. You can only imagine the surprise and glow this will create in them. Work with them if they ask you to change what you sent. The writer of the recommendation and the receiver both have the published recommendation posted on their respective LinkedIn profile pages. Everyone is served well.

- How many recommendations? I offer you my own Halpert Rule: the number of recommendations you receive and show on your LinkedIn profile should equal about 2% times the number of good, solid connections you have made. Too many makes you look cheesy; too few makes you look speculative. Approximately 2% seems to be just right. 3% may work better for you. Note: there is no ideal hard number of the recommendations you show. My rule seems to make empirical sense after all these years.

- **Connections:** These are your admirers, your colleagues, your confidantes, your surrounding crowd of support. Cull through the connections you have made over the years and reduce this list to people you have gotten to know through business, whom you trust, respect, and want to be seen in their company. Cultivate them.

  - You can, and should, disconnect from the ones who did not bear fruit or seem mistaken now; they will not receive any notification you deleted them. The resulting elite group is one from whom you can learn and to whom you can contribute. Make it a two-way nurturing relationship, creating a personal learning network, and everyone benefits.

- On-board new connections with an article or a special note every so often to keep them "sticky," as I call it. Then you are memorable with a positive, immediate impression in the early stages of a relationship, giving the new connection a sense of what will follow.

- Make LinkedIn the best of the available social media for your business pursuits by giving it more than you receive. I certainly don't need to impress upon you nonprofit pros the importance of paying it forward.

- **Followers:** Take notice of the people who come across your personal and/or your company profile page and want a middle ground: not to be connections, not to be strangers, but rather, they "follow" you to receive updates of articles you curated, your latest successes and news. Since you have no control over who follows you on LinkedIn, there is no way to vet them or delete them, so concentrate on nurturing your direct connections instead. Followers will benefit as a result.

- **Groups** are special interest silos of professionals on LinkedIn who aggregate around a topic: Online Fundraising for Nonprofit Organizations, Nonprofit Northeast, and LinkedIn Nonprofit Solutions, to name a few. I suggest you explore these groups of fellow experts and pose open-ended questions to gain the benefit of the group's combined knowledge. You don't know everything about your field and can learn from others' content. And answer others' questions too. Groups are ripe areas of low-hanging expertise waiting to be plucked.

- **Companies** (nonprofit organizations as well) can, and should, set up a micro website on LinkedIn called (and perhaps a misnomer for nonprofits) "company profile pages."

  - LinkedIn provides a comprehensive website to instruct nonprofits how to create their company profile pages. Take heed of their suggestions:

  https://nonprofit.linkedin.com/content/
  me/nonprofit/en-us/get-started/
  build-your-presence

  - Ask friends, employees, board members, and colleagues to click the "follow" button on your organization's company profile page. Every time your organization makes a change or addition to its company profile page, a LinkedIn message informs the followers. The admin on your staff responsible for the company page should take this seriously and can post news, list open job positions, consulting needs, press releases of new developments, and content to build relationships with your various stakeholders. If the content is rich and engaging, using graphics, photos, and videos, the automatic effect is to highlight your organization's work to other business professionals, attract them to your cause, and educate them about it. End each item with a call to action, like a URL to "donate now."

- If you are in a branch of a national nonprofit, be sure to contact the admin on the parent organization's company profile page before you set up one of your own. Cohesiveness among the federated chapters of the national organization is essential. The result: all voices in unison, as much as possible, for maximum brand effectiveness.

> • Be sure to feature the LinkedIn logo, and behind it the link to your LinkedIn company profile page, on all your marketing materials, business cards, website, email, etc. Make it easy for business professionals who are adept at using LinkedIn to find out more about you and your organization all at once while LinkedIn is open on their screen.

Recommendations, Connections, Followers, Groups, Companies: as you can see we are departing the purely "you" and we are already blending into the next section of this book: "us."

"You" and "Us"

You are a member of "us." All people in your organization, as a component of "us" must portray themselves according to the best practices I outlined above. One weak link can compromise the chain. I encourage each of "you" to be the best individually on LinkedIn and become a cohesive group of "us", that outsiders, "them," will admire.

The takeaways from this section about you:

- Be yourself and speak to the reader as if you are speaking directly to him or her.
- Be truthful, yet create the enhanced aura of marketing around your actions, word-smithing your profile so it stands out, to be "amazing-er" than the competition.
- Employ graphics, videos, slide decks, and other tools to complement your writing and make your overall profile more memorable.
- Illuminate, articulate, and cogitate a few editions of each section, highlight the best of each, amalgamate and edit into a narrative, one section amplifying and complementing the others, upwards and downwards, in your revised profile.
- Nothing is written in stone, so make changes to, and keep your personal profile up to date with, your activities and successes. Tell us so we know your path is heading onward and upward.
- Stay memorable by sharing material you think is especially worthwhile: others' articles, with your comments on why they are timely; original essays that we can all relate to, establishing you as a

thought leader in your connection base. Ask questions, answer them too, be an active participant among other great people you nurture.

- Make your network your net worth: vet prospects, seed new ones, cull out some that did not thrive, and cultivate and cross-pollinate the best ones.

- Recommend and endorse skills you know others have perfected, and ask for the reciprocal. Never let an accolade or a high compliment go undocumented or incorrectly stated.

- Finally, make LinkedIn an integral part of your brand, to leave an impression and make a memorable impact of "you."

Us

Colleagues, coworkers, vendors, advisors, consultants, volunteers, Board members (past, current, and prospective)…even established donors, generous corporate sponsors, past grantors, committed planned givers: *in general, all supporters and sympathizers to your organization*

Prologue

You have a lofty vision for a better future, but you cannot possibly accomplish this alone; your undertaking needs cohorts. Like eradicating a disease, forever preserving the habitat of a wild animal, or assisting new immigrants in matriculating to our society, you can't do it alone. It takes a community of like-thinking, active individuals.

Like eradicating a disease or forever preserving the habitat of a wild animal, or assisting new immigrants in matriculating to our society, you can't do it alone. It takes a community of like-thinking, active individuals.

But to the casual reader of the "us" LinkedIn profiles, does this group affinity come across cohesively? And does each person in the organization tell their part of the group game plan, according to their past/present/future career and their own lens? Do the profiles work as a group, too?

Because readers have limited attention spans, the message that the organization is united behind its mission must come across rapidly and concisely. Readers do not want to think too hard. They need the facts, passions, and reasons to support your cause, and to make that decision quickly. That means rich wording, convincing graphics and video, and a call to action, all in one place, and you can succeed in doing so on LinkedIn.

I already persuaded you that having a personal narrative on LinkedIn that outlines your career path to the position you play today in your organization is key to mapping your background: trusted and respected, a worker for the cause. You made the grade by spending the time and gaining experience. Your story covers your past, present, and future.

Your colleagues should describe their career paths, as well.

One by one, and in your own words, all of you unite around a commitment to make something important much better. Don't let your organization chance that some profiles are good and others not. That doesn't work well for attention-deficit stakeholders.

Plan and collaborate to reflect all of you, individually and as a team, as representing the organization you believe in. Be organized and deliberate in how and what you and your colleagues say on your personal profiles. A responsible marketing manager can play the role as the overarching creative force to knit all the individual stories together.

Plan and collaborate to reflect all of you, yet individually, and as a team, to represent the organization you believe in. Be organized and deliberate in how and what you and your colleagues say on your personal profiles.

Tell us.

The challenge for your brand marketing is to ensure a casual reader of your and your colleagues' profiles absorbs the story in the way the organization wants to be seen: a committed group of professional individuals who bring their cause to the forefront, in a cohesive voice, in ways supporters willingly contribute to.

Just Who Else Constitutes "Us"?

Beyond the obvious coworkers in your office, "us" is those who already support you and your cause, the cohort you incorporate into your personal LinkedIn profile, those of your coworkers, and the LinkedIn company profile of your organization.

"Us" comprises a range of people, all complementing the mission of your organization. Let's look at some of these supporters; as you do so, think: "what makes them react, help, and contribute," and I will provide some LinkedIn marketing techniques:

- colleagues
- vendors
- advisors
- consultants
- volunteers
- Board members (past, current, and prospective)
- the Executive Director too!

Note: In the next chapter we will look at targets like donors, corporate sponsors, grantors, and planned givers. They are external ("them") until they sign on with you in some way and then they become part of "us" (internal).

- **Colleagues** can include your networking connections, chamber-of-commerce neighbors, other nonprofit association colleagues, consultants who actively bring you the market's best ideas, and other associates with whom you collaborate on LinkedIn. They are enthusiastic cheerleaders for your thoughts and creativity, as you update them with curated articles you enjoyed enough to pass along with your commentary. And vice versa.

Ask them to connect on LinkedIn as your privilege of being associated with them. Or "follow" them on LinkedIn if something is preventing you from connecting to them. Think about each potential relationship carefully and your desire to be seen as associated with the individual: either follower or connection.

Fortunately, you and your co-workers all generate energy around a common bond. It starts at the top, from the Executive Director (ED) and the Board members. Each has his or her own area of expertise, responsibility, and goals as an experienced professional taking pride in completing group projects, one step towards completing the mission statement. Each has an entourage of support and influence. Some of these may overlap, some may complement, some may plow fresh terrain.

No one can do this alone; rather all of you in the organization, top to bottom, "rowing the boat in the same direction" as I like to say, take aim at a short-term accomplishment, one after another, each a step closer to your overall goals and vision. Ensure everyone in the organization is connected to one another on LinkedIn. Be active in supporting each other by sharing material and comments on successes. Be a championship team.

- **Vendors** can, and should, be among your greatest fans. After all, they have something to gain as you succeed and grow. Vendor relationships are worthy of nurturing via social media, too. If you truly like certain of your vendors, refer them for business to others. Endorse their skills. Tell us why you recommend the best ones on LinkedIn; tell a story about how they went above and beyond to support your cause. It's reasonable to approach them to support your next fundraising effort, too. What goes around comes around, right? Don't just think "corporate sponsorship;" reward it on social media, LinkedIn in particular!

- **Pro bono advisors** provide their expertise to you to ensure you thrive and succeed. The skills they contribute to your organization are worthy of your endorsement or recommendation on LinkedIn, as a direct payback for their professional expertise. Do not fail to make meaningful introductions to other potential clients using LinkedIn as well, to increase their business circle to your respected connections.

- **Consultants** to nonprofits are a group dear to my heart: I am one. I surround myself with many other experts whom I can refer with confidence to assist a nonprofit client in nearly any way imaginable, with superior performance. That's the net worth of my network, of course. You can connect on LinkedIn to your own consultants and even to those you did not ultimately contract with, but who impressed you in some measure. Collect a stable of experts to meet your needs, nurture them on LinkedIn, and tap into them when next needed.

- **Volunteers** are unsung heroes and sometimes invisible or underappreciated. Yes, you say "thank you" to them and reward then in other ways, such as an appreciation luncheon. But are you connected to them on LinkedIn? Do you continually and routinely acknowledge them by name in a LinkedIn update on your profile page or the company profile page for your organization? To do so, call them out in the body of the LinkedIn update with an "@" before their name and click on their LinkedIn persona, and they get a direct mention that travels to all their connections as well. Everyone looks great having done this! Encourage them to elaborate on the work they perform at your organization on their personal LinkedIn profile Volunteer Experience section. More eyes on your mission.

- The right **Board members** can be challenging to find. LinkedIn's search function allows you to set various search criteria to find the right person(s) with the credentials, in a specific location, with the skills and experience that will round out your Board. This creates a short list of candidates with credentials and experiences easy to review in one place. Searching for, and researching the background of, potential Board members is easy, and expected today. LinkedIn provides you a wealth of data and insight into each candidate, their rolodexes, their experience, their intertwined associations with funders, donors, and prospective stakeholders. Encourage the current Board members to identify what they contribute to the Board on their personal LinkedIn profile in the Volunteer Experience section. Additionally, creating a LinkedIn Group just for Board members allows communication among them only, admitted to the Group by invitation, and all correspondence is secure. Since the Board member is already using LinkedIn daily in his or her business, it's natural to add a Board-members-only LinkedIn Group for their exclusive use; or even for the use of one of its committees. I know of one private school that set up a Group including its executive staff and working parents to facilitate internal communication.

- The **Executive Director** sets the tone for all aspects of the organization: among them, its market image and social media face, LinkedIn included. The ED is often

> the public voice and communicator, so a reader or the press or a donor who visits the ED's LinkedIn personal profile page can glean the right imagery and message in all aspects of the organization's success. The ED needs to be fully involved and supportive of all levels' LinkedIn profiles. That branding commitment must start at the top.

Making these diverse groups part of your organization is key. Knitting these trusted supporters into your LinkedIn profile revalues them as a greater "us." Again, with effort and perseverance, LinkedIn will become a power tool in bringing the organization further together, from the outsider's point of view.

Making an "Us" for the World to Admire

Here are some ideas for making a company profile page work best for your organization, with personality and interest; while these take work and dedication, they can pay off:

- Announce your company profile page launch, and later, any substantive changes to it, to all employees.

- Urge staff members to "follow" your company profile page. Collect followers outside your organization too: volunteers, members, community officials, etc.

- Ask these followers to urge their connections to follow your company profile page, too.

- Remind them to share company page updates through their individual LinkedIn networks (to inform those who do not follow the company profile page).

- Invite employees to add their own accomplishments or project descriptions at kickoff time, etc., to the company profile page (the company profile admin should review all input for consistent messaging and branding). This gives you an organic source of content for your page.

- On-board new employees, Board members, and volunteers by asking them to follow your LinkedIn company profile page.

- Encourage Board members, donors, and volunteers to follow the company profile page and have them ask their connections to do so.

- Be consistent and energetic in adding new material to the company profile page to enhance its interest level and make it a stopping place for others: your annual report, photos from the gala, videos of your work in action, press releases, profiles of selected beneficiaries of your work, news of grants awarded, etc. In other words, if you put content on your website's news page, put it on your LinkedIn company profile page, too.

- Maintain a content calendar to keep this effort part of your marketing routine. Make each month reflect a theme and add material weekly.

- Share anecdotes, features, and human-interest stories of your social impact and give light to your organization's culture, especially if it is a heartwarming story and about one person making a difference.

- Tweet out a teaser to link back to your company profile page.

- Send a Facebook message as well, with the link to follow the LinkedIn company profile page.

Social media intertwines communities. With time, your actions will multiply followership and add more eyes to other efforts, enriching the whole organization.

Finally, keep all social media fresh, not just LinkedIn: revise as needed, add new material of interest to readers (know your audience) and remember that different generations prefer different forms of social media, absorbing new information on different social media platforms at varying times and frequencies of exposure.

Employees automatically become associated with the company profile page when they select the company profile page as their employer in their Experience sections. Take advantage of this membership. Show job openings, and recruit for Board and volunteer positions on your company profile page. Keep followers apprised of your need for and success in acquiring wish-list items, or show a thermometer of success to the funding goal. Members of your organization will find creative uses for the company profile page once they become familiar with it.

Keep followers apprised of your need for, and success in acquiring wish-list items, or show a thermometer of success to the funding goal.

And be sure to delete former employees from the company profile page by reminding them to key in the end date of their employment in their Experience section. You may ask them to continue to follow the company profile page, though.

Other underused aspects of the company profile page include creating "Showcase" subpages to highlight certain projects, drives, and events and accentuate mentions in the news, press releases, announcements of staff promotions, etc. Think: "hold-the-date" for events, links to register for your fundraisers, and wrap-ups after an event. Introduce and welcome new staff. Your organization can show anything your company profile page admin(s) decides is appropriate to promote. A company profile is your organization's free podium to LinkedIn's community of high-networth business professionals: real-time, editable, flexible, and graphics friendly.

For a treasure trove of more great marketing ideas, see LinkedIn's "Company Pages Playbook" at

https://business.linkedin.com/
marketing-solutions/blog/linkedin-
company-pages/2017/introducing-the-
linkedin-company-pages-playbook

See Us in Action: Video for the Organization

Video seems to cut across most generational and educational strata and is highly memorable.

You can benefit your cause using rehearsed, polished video shot and edited by a qualified videographer. Prepare and hone the message, the audio, and the visuals. You know what to put forth

> *Video seems to cut across most generational and educational strata and is highly memorable.*

from a quality organization such as yours, and how to compete with other organizations. Kick yours up a notch.

You may also want to consider a group-oriented video so all who appear in it can use the end-product on their personal profiles. Then you spread the same theme equally across multiple profiles. Simple? In concept. Completing this is the trick, but it is possible with a professional videographer's talent.

Or you can consider sporadic use of what the AV industry calls "native video" for a more spontaneous effect to share with your audience. LinkedIn makes native video available on their smartphone and tablet app. Nothing is more attention-grabbing than being in the moment with your smartphone and recording a brief video message to your followers and connections. Used sparingly and effectively, it puts the viewer in the moment and makes an impact.

Just be sure not to overdo using video! Be professional. You know how.

Donors and Supporters are Fickle

You are always competing for the same donor dollars with the organization down the hall or across town, or in the same delivery to a donor's postal mailbox or email box, especially at year end. That means donors can lose interest in your cause arising from a faulty perception, a poor impression, a less-than-memorable observation they make, bad press, or an opinion they hold. And they will not likely give you another chance.

I promise more on "them" later. Back to "us."

In the initial nanoseconds you get to make a good first impression via your social media profile, LinkedIn especially, personally and as a group, you must be perceived as a well-oiled collaborative effort, with some room allowed for individuality, personal creativity, and rich narrative.

Corporations and professional firms I work with struggle with the dichotomy: similar overall message from different professional personalities, all rolled together, so the reader is swayed towards pursuing your goals. In your nonprofit's case, perhaps your goal is a major or recurring gift.

Hard? Yes, it is.

Impossible? Not at all!

It takes work, revision, testing, trial balloons, more revision. It starts with the Executive Director or Board and trickles throughout. It requires an in-house administrative marketing referee: while being yourselves, all aim to be exciting to the most readers possible. Continual improvement will come by keeping the material relevant and up-to-date with the organization's news and funding successes.

Alluded to above, many organizations maintain a content calendar to reflect that month's theme; employees may be assigned to be the producer of content at the appointed time and topic, but the social media voice must be continuous and consistent. Maintain an interesting and regular content schedule. If it lapses, the reader may perceive the content is frozen in time, no longer relevant. That perception may extend to your organization.

Some of my clients have set aside a drive on their server to maintain a library of articles, news stories, white papers, client stories, and press releases that all employees can access to share on LinkedIn, individually and as an organization. Coupled with a tight person-

Some of my clients have set aside a drive on their server to maintain a library of articles, news stories, white papers, client stories, and press releases that all employees can access to share on LinkedIn, individually and as an organization.

al profile, these pre-approved, shared narratives and articles go a long way toward keeping each individual and the organization as a whole continually in the eyes, minds, and hearts of donors. Yes, there will always be late breaking news items or events; these can be spotlighted alongside the preapproved subject matter in the shared drive's library of materials.

Experiment and Excel

As you can see, you speak as part of many parties on LinkedIn, and while this may seem daunting, it is an exercise to take very seriously, and with practice, you will perfect it over time. You'll enjoy it especially as you layer on successes.

LinkedIn, too, is always changing. More methods of interaction become available over time as LinkedIn adjusts the service: never completed and always in transition.

Just like you.

Just like your organization.

Just like your donors.

Keep morphing. There's still time to make your organization look the best it can on LinkedIn to the professionals out there who have yet to become aware of the fine work performed by you and your colleagues in the organization for your constituency.

Now let's concentrate on attracting "them," i.e., those you have yet to meet or persuade to give. There are several methods for that on LinkedIn, too.

Them

Bringing the outsiders and
the fence sitters into your fold:
*expanding your organization by bringing
new people into your work*

Prologue

You want exposure and publicity. You crave attention for your cause. That does not come easily.

You want exposure and publicity. You crave attention to your cause. That does not come easily.

You work hard to be on the radar screen of the press as a nonprofit organization making a difference. You revel in word-of-mouth referrals.

You marvel at donations from first-time donors. Sometimes people wander in the door...or call unexpectedly and offer a $10,000 donation on the afternoon of December 31. Not too often, though.

More frequently, suppose an as-yet unknown donor, potential Board member, pro bono advisor, or grantor did their LinkedIn research and wanted to know about those individuals in your office making what you do so well all happen?

And your name came up? Along with others in your organization, above, laterally, and below you in seniority? Or the organization was noticed?

If they got this far, what next? Let's focus on "them" and their needs, not yours or your organization's.

Make Them At Least Fall in "Like" With You

Make it easy for them to find you on LinkedIn and read your and your colleagues' personal profiles, and / or the company profile page, so they are attracted enough to even consider donating their time, expertise, or funds!

I won't naively presume LinkedIn is the sole catalyst for an unexpected gift. But by now you recognize that you need to optimize it as one of the main marketing power tools in your toolbox to attract professionals to your cause.

Donors take multiple steps and make emotional decisions before they commit to give. LinkedIn can tune you to the donor, as the predominant social media for higher-net-worth business professionals, enhancing the process to learn more quickly, in one place, and better convincing the donor of your organization's need.

Business people are very likely already proficient in using LinkedIn to establish an initial reference point on you and your colleagues; as casual readers of your profile, they need to be comfortable with you on multiple planes:

> *Donors take multiple steps and make emotional decisions before they commit to give. LinkedIn can tune you to the donor, as the predominant social media for higher-net-worth business professionals.*

- How are you perceived in a first impression? Why you?

- How does the reader share common ground, colleagues, and perceptions with you and the executive staff?

- What news and values about your organization has the reader absorbed? Why (plural) you?

- Why should a reader feel good about helping you and your organization?

Be sure you individually and as an organization can answer "why" and "how" for the casual user, going beyond "who" or "what." At a higher level of understanding, "why" is the key to successfully articulating a reason for the process of following, participating, and donating. This "why" tips the reader into becoming a believer.

I did promise to focus on "them" in this section, but I want to remind you that you will not get them to read your profile, and your colleagues' and/or the organization's profile, unless you stir curiosity, play upon interests, and thus compel the reader to take in the need you serve. Full circle: them, back to you and us.

But first more detail on the various parties that make up "them."

Donors

The fact that LinkedIn users have a higher net worth, beyond users of most other social media platforms, is the most compelling reason to optimize your organization's outbound branding message on LinkedIn. Potential donors are all over LinkedIn, 146+ million in the USA at this writing, and it is probably safe to say you have yet to engage even a small percentage of them!

Make your presence and need known by your smart, professional use of LinkedIn, consistently and continuously marketing the brand. Speak to this exclusive audience, not at them: they are savvy professionals who can be persuaded to help you further your cause. The "pay it forward" theme is pervasive in social media. So your use of LinkedIn needs to speak to this successful and highly educated audience in a different tone than your website, Facebook page, and/or Twitter handle. Convince them why "you" and "us".

The frequency and diversity of your touchpoints with donors are limited by your imagination. Make them want to open your newest update, pre-advise them of what they are about to see or read in a video or article you post, and lay out "why" from your point-of-view.

The frequency and diversity of your touchpoints with donors is limited by your imagination. Make them want to open your newest update on LinkedIn.

It is important for them to spend the time in reading or watching your material.

Post a PDF of your Form 990, your annual report, and your news on your LinkedIn company profile page, so potential donors can review the year's accomplishments and the organization's financial state. Retell success stories that stir the imagination and warm the heart; celebrate the end-results of your mission's work, one case at a time. Show pictures, video, and other graphics to give context and make a visual image a lasting memorable one. Be fascinating.

Persuading smart people to part with their money is an art! Persuading business pros to do so is a fine art, in my estimation.

Corporate Sponsors

Straddling the for-profit and the nonprofit sectors, these corporate decision-makers are closely tied to LinkedIn in their business lives and, for those who volunteer, in their personal lives. By searching and vetting referrals from common connections, then nurturing them in new relationships, you will find opportunities to attract nearby corporate sponsorships you never knew possible, nurtured for the foreseeable future.

But your challenge is to impress corporate giving managers with your business social media savvy and keep them salivating, as well. Then they more readily consider taking a gold level ad page in your gala journal, bidding for a big-ticket auction item, reserving a full table (or more!) at your gala, sponsoring your event, or making a big-dollar gift to help you reach your higher goals, all in concert with their corporation's charitable vision. Speak to this audience with the right frequency and context on LinkedIn.

> *Your challenge is to impress corporate giving managers with your business social media savvy and keep them salivating, as well.*

Grant Decision Makers

Grant administrators are perhaps the most mysterious funding decision-makers. Your grant application, complete and cogent, no matter how deserving you believe you are, is often given a black-and-white decision by unseen grant makers. Again, it's your goal to impress and entice that foundation to

> *It's your goal to impress and entice a foundation to sustain the success of your organization, and that makes LinkedIn an even more important social medium.*

sustain the success of your organization, and that makes LinkedIn an even more important social medium input to encourage the grant decision makers to consider you so worthy of their funding, especially with so many other organizations competing against you for the same money.

Grant writers I know tell me that reviewing your LinkedIn presence is not quite standard, but may become an incremental fact in awarding a grant, and by extension, receiving another one the year thereafter. If a direct competitor is anemic in its LinkedIn persona, and you are not, perhaps, just perhaps, this might tip the money flow your way. Isn't LinkedIn worth that effort? Even if not asked for your LinkedIn URL, or that of your organization, offer it anyhow, especially if you are telling the story in a different way.

Planned Giving

Until you land the commitment of a planned gift from the donor, you need to work diligently in building your relationship before, during, and after every "touch" you have with them.

And not just them individually; you can influence a family member or a trust attorney who appreciates your mission and sees you demonstrating best practices on LinkedIn. Then they can research you. They may refer you to a planned giver, based on their impression.

I am finding a keen interest in LinkedIn among planned giving consultants, financial planners, and attorneys as a way to educate their wealthy clients on worthy organizations, to encourage them to leave you part of their estate, their ultimate compliment. It takes a process and a marketing plan, but LinkedIn may spur the desired end result forward faster.

You can influence a family member or a trust attorney who appreciates your mission and sees you demonstrating best practices on LinkedIn. Then they can research you.

Skilled Professionals

Here's a gift from LinkedIn for your organization: LinkedIn allows you to attract skilled professionals and show how they can volunteer their services to your organization: pro bono expertise or Board membership. Post your needs at

https://www.linkedin.com/jobs

As a suggestion, post your open position and start the title and description with "Volunteer" or "Board

Member" to receive the best results from your listing. On the opposite side of the equation, professionals can list pro bono skills they offer local nonprofits and/or signify interest in serving on a Board in their LinkedIn personal profiles. Then they are matched to the open position you listed when you search for them.

Professionals can list pro bono skills they offer local nonprofits and/ or signify interest in serving on the Board in their LinkedIn personal profiles.

It's a marketplace for pro bono expertise. On the right-hand side, select one or both under Nonprofit Interests: Skilled Volunteering or Board Service:

https://www.linkedin.com/search/
results/people/

See? LinkedIn is a search engine here, as well as a job board and a marketing machine where you elevate your organization concurrent with its needs.

The Press

Be available to journalists sympathetic to your cause and covering news as you feed it to them.

The news industry relies on LinkedIn as a concise, one-stop source of information on the personalities who are movers and shakers in the stories they cover. That's your ED, you, your Board members, and your colleagues telling why you each and together are so impassioned in what you do, what your goals are, and how you envision a brighter future to the reader of your LinkedIn profile.

In today's never-ending cycle of information flow, cajoling the local and industry press reporters is essential. We have moved beyond issuing a press release and expecting the newspaper to copy it into the local events section. Today, reporters seek expertise in specific, narrow areas of knowledge. If they are to find you as that source, it may just be via a LinkedIn search using the keywords from their story topic that identifies you as an expert.

Conversely, the electronic press is hungry for original material. If you have a point of view to share and write it well, submit it in expectation of establishing a new place for others to find your expertise. Update your connections with a few lines announcing your article and the URL linking them to it. Memorialize this publication, and any others in which you are author, are featured, are quoted, etc., in the

If you have a point of view to share and write it well, submit it in expectation of a new place for others to find your expertise.

Publications section of your LinkedIn personal profile. Be sure the company profile of your organization showcases your work, too. Keep submitting once you are published. Be a thought leader to the press. More eyes on your mission, right? Donors read and digest the news in any form it takes.

Rating Agencies and Watchdogs

The image that donors and evaluators of your organization receive from the handful of rating agencies protecting the public is immeasurable and important.

Do not forget that rating agencies peruse many published sources of information in making their determination. Perhaps they will look at you and your organization on LinkedIn, not just at financial data.

Mention your ratings. Keep them up-to-date. They help others make up minds: donations, Board seats, expertise, etc.

Being clear and direct in your LinkedIn personal profile and the company profile of the organization is essential, as stated above.

Local Community

And let's not forget how pleased the local community is to have you in their midst, whether your mission is helping them and/or surrounding communities, or just the fact that smart and giving people add to the quality of the population. The nonprofit pros are probably PTA officers, local volunteers in time of crisis, experts in a topic that must be brought in from outside, those who call out a problem that is burgeoning before it gets impossible to solve, etc.

When partnering with other organizations in your community, ensure they project a brand image on LinkedIn and other social media that matches your quality.

When partnering with other organizations in your community, ensure they project a brand image on LinkedIn and other social media that matches your quality.

The public respects the work "you" do. As part of the community of "them," organize to bring a combined good image and name to "us."

Coopetition

There's a sea of other nonprofit professionals out there whose work in other organizations is similar to yours. Social media is built on the premise of "pay it forward," strangers helping one another. Not so much in business, more likely in the nonprofit sector on LinkedIn. I call this "coopetition" and suggest you try it.

You can tap into these nonprofit pros individually; the best way to find the right ones to collaborate with and gain the benefit of their experience is through leveraging referrals from your existing LinkedIn connections.

Ask the connection to introduce you through LinkedIn to make this smoother, so the other party has a chance to review your role and credentials within the context of a mutual contact. Send a LinkedIn message or email referencing your LinkedIn profile URL and secure a date and time for your phone conversation.

Before you contact the referred competitor, ask the mutual connection how they plan to refer you. Pursue this so you understand how you are perceived: where is the common ground? Review the target's LinkedIn profile, their nonprofit's company profile page, its website, and its Facebook page. Be prepared when you contact the competitor to make the time efficient and well spent.

Have the competitor's LinkedIn profile page open on your screen when you call. It's more natural for speaking, using cues from their past, present, and future to work into the conversation. Make it a great call. You never know where it may lead, if not immediately, then down the road. Follow up on any open items that were discussed and agree on a timetable for exchanges. Adhere to the agreed time to deliver and enhance your brand of reliability.

A thank you email or message via LinkedIn is also in order. Be sincere and warm.

(All this sounds obvious, right? Not everyone adheres to simple etiquette when introduced, so I mention this to remind you of some old-school ways that still make a difference.)

Finally, if you feel the other person may provide additional connectivity and benefit (and it's a two-way street!), invite him or her to connect to you on LinkedIn. Send a personalized invitation to connect, reminding how you met and when and what you discussed, providing context, in case they do not open your connection request immediately.

On-board them as a newly-hatched LinkedIn connection: within the same week send an article you believe will benefit them as a token of appreciation for the privilege a LinkedIn connection truly is. Keep nurturing them.

Think of others to introduce them to within your network, mindful to make thoughtful and meaningful connections that will always reflect well on you.

Offer to meet the new connection for coffee, a meal, or before a conference, and ask that person to follow your organization on its LinkedIn company profile page.

In your mind, start them as a referred coopetitor, then cooperator, then colleague, then friend and business advisor — all relationships start somewhere and can mature into a trusted, valued assembly of the best-in-class in your field, with quality effort on both parts.

Coopetition is one way to make valued connections outside your organization that you can tap into as needed. Expect to reciprocate; offer to do so, as well.

Pay it forward, even if you are always busy. Share the wealth of knowledge in special purpose personal learning networks on LinkedIn.

Coopetition is one way to make valued connections outside your organization that you can tap into as needed. Expect to reciprocate; offer to do so, as well.

Take the time now, while the situation is fresh in your mind, to inquire and/or invest in knowledge from your colleagues. Use LinkedIn to share ideas, successes, and approaches to solving problems with your entourage of friendly competitors, reliable collaborators, and trusted advisors. Increase your network's net worth to you, and conversely, yours to them.

Embrace the Challenge

Each of the "them" has something you want or need, and while you may think of yourself as worthy of the initial attraction, you need to entice them to start, albeit slowly, with you. Keep them continuously interested, professionally ramping up the interaction over time. You cannot count on their donation or action until you persuade them.

Keep them continuously interested, professionally ramping up the interaction over time. You cannot count on their donation or action until you persuade them.

You may not succeed upon first introduction; it is a courtship, of course. As you now know, LinkedIn affords you a few unique ways to "ping" on the target's mental radar: articles you share, essays you post, comments/questions/answers in Groups, messages directly to them, recommendations bestowed by mutual colleagues, and the all-powerful who-knows-whom in the interpersonal network on which LinkedIn sheds new light.

Nurture these decision makers on LinkedIn; be visible and memorable in doing so. There is continual competition for the outside party's attention, money, and loyalty. Government and private grants are shrinking and becoming even more competitive. That leads a nonprofit back to LinkedIn's unique participation by corporate sponsors and corporate professionals at all demographic and geographic locations and experience levels.

I will assume you agree at this point that your personal profile, organizational messages, and brand need to be consistent and increasingly interesting, so much so that the goal is enmeshing these third parties in you and your organization's mission for participation in various new, enriching ways.

You, Us, Them, Conclusion

You: One person making a difference, telling us what's dear to you and meaningful in your work, as only you can. Appear the best you can be on LinkedIn, approachable and active, so we can cheer you on as you achieve your next milestones. Be sure your personal LinkedIn profile fits within the intentions of your nonprofit organization's brand.

Us: The power of the group's coordinated message, inspiring and successful. The message to the business community on LinkedIn must be on-point and concise, everyone in the organization showing a side of the mission in their individual profiles, with no weak links.

Them: All kinds of people who have not yet contributed to your cause but are available to you to research and selectively market to. When they are inspired by your cause, they offer you their expertise, time, and money. On LinkedIn, they are businesspeople and business entities: attention-deprived, questioning, and return-on-investment-driven. Appeal to both their intellect and their emotional desire to help, as we all pay it forward.

Are the three incompatible? Not if you work on LinkedIn using the concepts I showed you.

Cohesive? Certainly. This will take work, but it is attainable. Feed and cultivate it continually.

Collaborative? Ah, the best of all worlds, all three rowing the boat in the same direction.

Made You Think

The purpose of this book, as stated in the introduction, is to make you aware of LinkedIn marketing concepts that you as a nonprofit professional can bring back to your organization and use to help evangelize individually and together, expressing *why you* (singular and plural) to sway a third party to join your cause.

In writing this book, I may have enlightened you, and hopefully you gleaned many new ideas that you can draw on and optimize for your needs. I may have caused some introspection, and with that, angst.

In any event, it's a good idea to stretch and self-examine occasionally as a professional. It's a best practice to continually invest in yourself, in your brand. It's important to make midcourse corrections as needed to hone your talking points, in various places in different contexts, so the casual third-party reader or donor, etc. "gets" why you do what you do, what you stand for, and whose company you keep.

Only you can tell us. Make the most of it.

I hope you will look at my online LinkedIn course for nonprofit professionals that will give you the nuts and bolts, play-by-play of how to mechanically set up your LinkedIn profile. This book is a reference guide to why you say what you do and how you say it. You can read about the course and register at

https://connect2collaborate.wordpress.com

The course complements this book. And vice versa. Together, the book and course set you up to present yourself and your nonprofit organization in an optimal light.

Please advise me of any feedback you have and especially success stories you can share along the way.

Of course, I appreciate hearing how this book helps you in your career future.

Changes on LinkedIn occur without notice. This book is considered correct as of its publication. If you find otherwise, I would appreciate hearing from you to make the next edition that much better and helpful for you.

Please let me hear your successes using my concepts. That would provide me the satisfaction of a book well written.

Finally, please subscribe to my free LinkedIn blog, where I post my thoughts and observations, with a LinkedIn twist, every business day. You can subscribe at

> https://connect2collaborate.wordpress.
> com/todays-linkedin-nugget/

Make an even bigger difference using LinkedIn as a power tool in your toolbox.

Case
Studies

Interviews with nonprofit professionals
who use LinkedIn well

Bill Brucker, Kristin Sinatra, and Hugh Reilly generously provided their expertise and keen observations when I interviewed them for this book. Each is a successful marketing professional with in-depth understanding of the nonprofit sector and an experienced user of LinkedIn for promoting their own branding and that of their organization.

Their comments resonated amazingly well with the intent of this book, even though I spoke with them after the manuscript was already in editing and graphic production.

They were emailed a set of questions to think about, which I would use for my 45-minute conversation with them. The sessions were audio recorded, and I gleaned the best to share with you as a means of stimulating new ideas and creative ways to market your brand, based on their successes. The highlights of their responses appear below.

While the mission, purpose, and size of the organizations they represent may not apply to you directly, I do believe there is utility in learning from those who have found wide success, so you can translate the ideas that they find work well into your specific situation.

Bill Brucker, Family Centers

Bill Brucker is an "award-winning communications pro, nonprofit strategic planner and marketing expert" (from his LinkedIn profile headline) and VP of Communications at Family Centers in Greenwich, CT:

https://www.linkedin.com/in/billbrucker/

Family Centers, from its LinkedIn company profile page "is a private, nonprofit organization offering education, health and human services to children, adults and families in Fairfield County...Through our three Centers of Excellence, children, adults, families and communities receive the care, encouragement and resources needed to realize their potential."

https://www.linkedin.com/company/135812/

Why do you, Bill, do what you do?

"Professionally, I have always had a cause-related need to do what I do. Being in communications, marketing and strategic planning, it's tough to find that balance. I started my career in the corporate world and learned so many valuable skills, but at the end of the day my work didn't benefit anyone other than a company's bottom line. I made the switch over to the nonprofit sector because it allowed me to hone my marketing and public relations experience and tell stories that impact people's lives. Working for an organization like Family Centers, I have the benefit of showcasing tremendous programs and services that benefit."

Why does Family Centers do what it does?

"I can help tell these stories and showcase these amazing programs so that our community can be stronger. That's what gets me excited when I wake up on a Monday morning — to know that in some small way the efforts that I'm doing will broaden the awareness and profile of Family Centers and its programs and have some impact on somebody's life who really needs our services."

...

"I tap into what I've learned in those other sectors to create a brand that has helped Family Centers not only expand its service delivery methodology but also help to bring in money and connect with donors and others in the community."

...

"You do need to have business acumen to really set yourselves apart from other organizations that are competing for the same philanthropic dollars and same public audiences that you're trying to reach. You need something to set yourself apart and I think having a strong branded marketing and awareness arm of an organization is crucial for that growth."

How do you keep Family Centers colleagues' messages on LinkedIn aligned with the overall themes you market?

"My department works closely with everybody on staff to reinforce that, even though I may be running the marketing function and overseeing the day-to-day. This is a partnership across the entire organization. We all have a role to play, so giving staff ideas on how they can deliver a consistent message across LinkedIn and other social platforms keeps that uniform brand. Family Centers has 25 different programs, and it's very easy for staff to get zoned in on the area in which they work. But the more education we do internally to let our staff know about the entirety of the organization allows them to be advocates in the community and on social media and other communication platforms. We really try to create a culture that speaks to the fact that we're all in this messaging together and that it's going to benefit all."

...

"I try to make it a point to get to know staff on every level because I look at what I do from a marketing and communications standpoint as a partnership. If I don't have the trust of, and a relationship with, everybody on staff to help carry our branding and our messaging

101

further, then you're sunk right out of the gate. I regularly meet with staff of the various departments and programs, just to check in and regularly beat the drum that lets us look beyond their particular program and constantly promote. We also have a new hire orientation where I let new staff know how they can be helpful in in our efforts as well, so it's really up to me."

...

"I may be the central repository for all the branding information, but I like to empower our team to be a part of it in terms of promoting events going on within the programs. I always tell our team that they are the experts. They're on the front lines, they see what's happening on a regular basis and I'm relying on them to guide me what they're seeing and what's important: take a picture, write a little blurb that we can use for various social media postings and be a part of it. I think having that level of empowerment gets them excited that they have a say in the messaging and the marketing because they really do have a sense of ownership over their own programs. I think they appreciate that that it's not just somebody from the executive team deciding what is best to say about their programs. They're invested, they're embedded in the messaging as well."

Who is your "them" and how do you use LinkedIn to inform and attract them?

"We have a number of different stakeholders that we're trying to engage with on a regular basis. Obviously, funders are our major audience that we're always looking to engage with and showcase the impact that we have in the community. Volunteers are a big piece of that audience, as well as community partners because we're working so closely with other organizations in the community on collective impact projects. We want to make sure that we're reaching out to them to a certain degree."

...

"When you look at all those different audiences I think various social media platforms appeal to them more than others. A good example: our donor base, and particularly members of our board, are very big into Instagram."

...

They do enjoy seeing pictures and highlights of what's happening, which might not be as appropriate for a forum like LinkedIn as it would be for Instagram. But I will say that anytime that we have something business-related that can really speak to the broader audience we certainly turn to LinkedIn."

"We've had some great success with using LinkedIn to promote our Titan fundraising series, which is focused on business-related speakers. From time to time we've had great success leveraging LinkedIn, and the people that are following us on LinkedIn, and we encourage our staff to share on LinkedIn as well, to fill the room, and that's been great."

...

"In terms of really broadening the awareness of that event, I think a lot of it had to do with the talent that we were bringing in. For one event a couple years ago, we brought in Federal Reserve Chairman Paul Volcker and we used LinkedIn as a primary way to promote the speech. We didn't do any kind of hard invitation. Knowing that we wanted to reach out to the business community, we did a lot of electronic marketing, LinkedIn being one of the primary venues."

...

"Sometimes we've used paid advertisements on LinkedIn to further awareness of our events, but I think when you hold something that that speaks to a particular sector you're trying to reach, and when you have a talent like Volcker, it was relatively easy."

...

"One of the other audiences that we are trying to attract, and where LinkedIn has been particularly useful, is new employees. Since we opened our health clinic about two years ago, it's a challenge to find specialized medical professionals to staff our clinics, in which we require very specific and specialized professional skills to keep our programs running. We've regularly used LinkedIn to reach out and let people know that these opportunities are available, while also leveraging our own staff in Family Centers to advise their own networks to broaden the message that we're looking for these specialized staff people. We've found some pretty good candidates from our LinkedIn efforts, and we toyed with the idea of a LinkedIn recruitment program."

...

"We put the CFO position out on LinkedIn this past winter, pushing out through various posts and we had a tremendous response so having a wide built-in audience on LinkedIn certainly helps with recruitment."

How do you get more results from corporate supporters, foundations, or organizations that are in our general area, and businesspeople who want to help with their pro bono expertise, specifically, with LinkedIn marketing in a way that you think is unique to your situation?

"Going beyond the relationships we've established, and the connections where we have a face-to-face personal relationship, we can certainly make inroads and expand the reach of the organization and connect with additional supporters. It's not solely data-driven marketing that works, but more of our donors and more of our supporters are looking for that kind of sound bite that they can hold on to and really understand in two seconds."

...

"I don't think that we really have scratched the surface using our data, testimonials, and the various ways to show our impact on LinkedIn. But I think as we further develop our strategy for our outreach, particularly around LinkedIn, we will see a tremendous amount of return as we further hone our LinkedIn strategy. That includes video. If you're not doing video, utilizing the human element on a visual medium, you're totally missing your audience. That's the way people are consuming information these days, getting right to the heartstrings and that's what you're looking to actually hit."

Bonus question: What's one surprise you've gotten through LinkedIn you didn't expect?

"What surprised me more than anything is how many unsolicited people are interested in following nonprofits like us on LinkedIn. For lack of a better word, we're a "feel good" organization: we're out there to make an impact, improve and elevate people's lives. What always surprises me when I check the metrics on

LinkedIn is how many people in the Fairfield County (Connecticut) business community follow us because they have an interest in the work we do. To me it's a great opportunity to use those followers and their connections to tap into their capacity to get involved, whatever it could be: financial, volunteer, advocacy. At the end of the day it's amazing and heartening to see how many professionals out there are looking for a philanthropic and community-minded aspect to their professional career, using LinkedIn to connect with the nonprofits and finding ways to personally make a difference in their communities."

Kristin Sinatra, Waveny LifeCare Network

Kristin Sinatra from her LinkedIn profile is "an intuitive marketing executive, brand strategist, SEO specialist, creative director, graphic designer, wordsmith and social media maven with a deft hand and strategic point of view." She provides marketing direction, strategy and insight as VP of Marketing at Waveny LifeCare Network in New Canaan, CT:

https://www.linkedin.com/in/ kristin-sinatra/6496a26

Waveny LifeCare Network, from its LinkedIn company profile page is a nonprofit that "offers a progression of therapeutic programs, services and living options to enhance the quality of life of those within our care:" independent senior living, assisted living for people with Alzheimer's and memory loss, skilled nursing, home healthcare, geriatric evaluation, geriatric care management, and an adult day program."

https://www.linkedin.com/company/1885287/

Why do you do what you do?

"For as long as I can remember, there's always been something in me that needs to serve a higher purpose. It's incredibly rewarding to help heighten awareness of a mission that I truly believe in, and I feel at my best when I know I'm using all of myself on behalf of something bigger than myself. Knowing that I can help guide people toward the best solutions to complex and challenging issues makes my role feel very important and validates every bit of myself I give to it."

Where did that come from? How long ago do you remember actually feeling that?

"I have my mother's heart and my father's brain. Believe it or not, my first career was actually in politics, where I was driven by this same calling to further important ideas, philosophies and ethics that I believed in. What is politics anyway, but marketing with a candidate as its product, and their platform as their mission? There's always been something in me that has wanted to further something truly noble from behind the curtain, so to speak. Transitioning out of politics to what I do now was very natural, because best practices in both fields revolve around the same core tenets — heightening awareness and underscoring unique points of difference."

...

"In both careers alike, I knew I was never cut out to market widgets. I'm a service-oriented marketer. In order to feel fulfilled, I need to know I'm helping to point people towards quality, and the best solutions to what they seek. I've served Waveny for 14 years now, and marketing our incredible organization is one of my biggest passions. I have such a deep connection to our mission and strong belief in the good work we do. To know that my job is to achieve the loudest megaphone possible for an organization that's committed to providing therapeutic and progressive solutions? Well, that's a privilege."

Why does Waveny do what it does?

"The short answer is that we do what we do for seniors and their families. But the longer answer is that we do what we do because we're tasked with it in a completely self-imposed way, by virtue of being a mission-driven organization. What should we do but to deliver upon our mission, and what is our mission but something that's 100% dedicated to people? So, if you transitively connect those dots, everything that we do is in the best interest of people. When I think about it, our mission is really the only responsible one a healthcare institution could have in this day and age. Because it hinges on adapting and evolving what we do, how we do it, and the services we provide, to meet the changing needs the seniors and their families. Change is constant, so we cannot stay stagnant. Instead, we task ourselves to be one step ahead at all times — not just to meet existing needs as they are today, but as they may be tomorrow."

How do you say Waveny's mission is different than the next best competitor?

"That's easy — the vast majority of our competitors aren't nonprofits and aren't mission-driven. We are a nonprofit provider in a sea of for-profit enterprises. We are an eldercare provider that's committed to providing a person-centered continuum of care, which is very different from the stand-alone assisted living communities that make up the bulk of eldercare providers out there."

For those of us who are very nonprofit-oriented I get that, but when a family is shopping for a place for mom, dad, etc., but how does a non-profit orientation differentiate from the next for-profit?

"Everything we do is based on quality and excellence, and sometimes we've been known to affectionately say that the seniors whom we serve are our "bottom line" — an obvious play on words about stockholders and profits. Our focus lies in providing the highest quality of care versus meeting corporate quotas. We make a promise to every senior who moves into any of Waveny's residences. We give them the assurance that they will have access to Waveny in its entirety — and moreover, priority access to our 5-star nursing home, Waveny Care Center — should their financial or care needs change."

...

"As a charitable organization, there is philanthropy at the heart of what we do. I think my favorite fund at Waveny is our Resident Assistance Fund, which provides financial support to defray costs and lessen the financial burden of those we serve, when their private funds diminish. If eventually that individual needs to go on Medicaid, they have the priority access to our 5-star skilled nursing facility. Being able to give seniors and their families the assurance of access to the world's best safety net provides a palpable sense of peace of mind."

How do you package that message and push it out there?

"In many ways. Our mission has tasked us with evolving into a continuum. That's a driving part of the Waveny difference. Marketing Waveny is a balance between heightening awareness of our collective continuum and leveraging the individual service lines within the context of that continuum, as well as the equity of the trusted Waveny name."

...

"Talking about our many points of difference as a nonprofit has everything to do with talking about being quality focused and person-centered. "Person-centered care" is not just a series of buzzwords or catchphrase we use; it's a way to convey that everything we do emphasizes the person first. We approach each person as the individual they are, from beginning to end. There are things that other eldercare providers like to dance around, namely the fact that finances are finite. When your focus is on providing excellence in care, the senior receiving that care can often outlive their finances — which speaks to the quality of the care itself. So again, communicating that we can care for someone regardless of how their financial or personal care needs may change, is at the heart of our messaging and helps us to stand apart. In terms of using LinkedIn, LinkedIn gives us a forum to tell an important story to the community, a story about who we are. It reinforces how solid our brand is."

Give me an example of success you really didn't expect that came through LinkedIn.

"Successes that come to mind immediately for me on LinkedIn hinge on access to professionals. I will often describe that marketing Waveny involved taking to several different audiences. As I've come to understand it, marketing eldercare involves a hybrid assortment of audiences. The first layer is the decision-maker versus the prospect of the patient--sometimes they're the same, but more often they're not. When they are not, it's usually the adult child versus a senior spouse."

...

"But there is another layer: we rely heavily on professional referrals. Without it being one of the more overt ways we use LinkedIn in marketing, business-to-business confidence is bred through our strategic use of social media. Beyond referrals, the quality we provide is only as good as the talent we employ and retain. LinkedIn is a powerful staff recruitment tool, and something taken into consideration by many people seeking to learn more about the professional environment we offer. It's one of the most frequently used channels of what I call "professional voyeurism," and our success is seen in these prospects continuing to pursue us, rather doing an immediate U-turn, after taking a private look at us on LinkedIn."

...

"In many positions, including management, prospective candidates try to "get to know us" on LinkedIn before applying or walking in the door. It's a go-to tool for professionals, and I believe that what they see us doing, and how they see us doing it, on LinkedIn speaks to our quality in general. It shapes how people see us before they know us. In today's digitally savvy society, I know with certainty that maintaining a high social media base does much more than allow an organization to grow its reach — that "megaphone" I mentioned previously. Beyond marketing a literal message, social media wields the ability to drill down to the subconscious and affect how people perceive us."

…

"The best kind of marketing that exists is word-of-mouth, hinging on a personal referral or testimonial. Any marketer who tells you otherwise should take a moment to pause and reflect on what they do, and why they do it. When you look at social media fellowship and following, and think about what it really is, you notice that it's really just another expression of word-of-mouth. It's a vote of confidence that couldn't be clearer."

…

"I often think about an article I read several years ago in the American Journal of Medical Quality called, "Do Patients 'Like' Good Care?" (http://journals.sagepub.com/doi/abs/10.1177/1062860612474839) It discussed a visible correlation between hospitals, numbers of Facebook likes, and their traditional quality indicators. The finding of a strong relationship between the two didn't surprise me at all. While this piece mainly concentrated on Facebook, I think the same holds true for LinkedIn. A strong presence on LinkedIn is a reflection of how serious you are as an organization. A strong LinkedIn presence – and demonstrating to the consumer that we're buttoned-up enough to know how to use it the appropriately in terms of netiquette and best practices — complements our credibility. It gives people looking at us a sense of confidence in us before they even know us. Whether conscious or subconscious, I'm certain that people view an organization's social media as a reflection of its credibility, and that is a reality that marketers should not try to escape."

How do you keep your colleagues' messages on point? I mean, clearly you have articulated a very lateral ability to keep everything tidy, on point, in marketing?

"Good question and I don't think it's a coincidence that you're asking me it at this juncture in time. Thinking about this question actually led me to determining one of my personal goals for this year. I'm in the process of developing a staff-wide in-service about best practices in using social media. Maintaining brand standards is something you can help manage and control through education."

...

"My strategy in practice now involves providing highly sharable content, so that proud staff members aren't compelled to create their own content — I spend a lot of time developing meaningful social media that can confidently be shared, without needing to polish, modify or personalize it."

How do market and approach "them" for Waveny?

"When I touched upon this earlier, I said there are four audiences that I market to and I think I stopped at the third tier — the consumers versus professionals. The fourth division is what I called the "planners versus the deniers." Planners make a point to learn and prepare for future needs proactively, but deniers wait until a crisis situation to undertake their education process in hyper speed, which is more often than not marked with desperation. So, being findable and well-positioned is essential. Care is local, so often an adult child's first instinct to seek help for their senior parents is to go online to research local solutions. Since we've been so digitally progressive, Waveny is easily findable through their searches. If they come across "Waveny," and seek to learn more about us specifically, there will be no shortage of positive content-rich results when they do. And due to LinkedIn's powerful, organic SEO, our LinkedIn page will be among the top results."

Who else is your "them"?

"Others seeking help and not knowing where to begin are often bound to ask their physicians or healthcare professionals for personal recommendations or referrals. Professional outreach is so important to what we do. We actually have a dedicated full-time community liaison who devotes her entire day to preaching our points of difference to the local clinical community. When a professional recommendation is made, and "Waveny" is on the receiving end of it, this is another juncture where an online investigative research process can begin. A different source to spark the online inquiry, but with the same patterns, behaviors, decision making and results following."

Hugh Reilly, UNICEF

Hugh Reilly is *"a talented and experienced digital leader, social media storyteller, marketing manager, web/youth trainer and qualified journalist...who established and cemented UNICEF's position as the largest international nonprofit/NGO organization on social media."* and Digital Communications Specialist at UNICEF in New York, NY (from his LinkedIn profile):

https://linkedin.com/in/hughreillygotme

UNICEF *"works in some of the world's toughest places, to reach the world's most disadvantaged children. To save their lives. To defend their rights. To help them fulfill their potential. Across 190 countries and territories, we work for every child, everywhere, every day, to build a better world for everyone. And we never give up."* (from its LinkedIn company profile page):

https://www.linkedin.com/company/4881/

As the Digital Communications Specialist at UNICEF with responsibility for the LinkedIn branding, how do you plan your content calendar? With so much to

say, how do you decide who's going to say what and how you are going to say it on LinkedIn?

"As background, we inherited a LinkedIn presence set up by our internal communications team, but it really wasn't being used much. We gained control of it as we increased our digital governance and planned to employ the best strategy for LinkedIn. We felt tailoring the content to a professional audience rather than the general public — which we do more on Facebook and Twitter — was important for us."

...

"The UNICEF brand is strong, and most people are warm to the brand. We were finding that the number one question, especially among the younger audience, was (and still is) "How can I work for UNICEF?" There is a gap in educating them about what different roles exist and what attributes you need to work in those roles."

Is the evolving intent of the LinkedIn company profile page filling jobs, education, or content, or a mix?

"Being audience driven, we developed our LinkedIn company profile to meet our audiences' needs. We share content revolving around our big priorities affecting children, Q&As with staff on our www.facesofunicef.tumblr.com, and other material with a professional work focus. Around the same time we launched a UNICEF blog,

http://blogs.unicef.org

with content written not only by communications professionals, but by subject-area expert staff covering a variety of issues, and that content, which is not necessarily appropriate for Facebook or Twitter, is pushed out on LinkedIn a couple of times a week. One of our goals on LinkedIn is humanizing the brand and putting a face to the work of UNICEF, since as part of the UN we may be perceived a bit bureaucratic and not transparent."

…

"Over the last year, we have been working more closely with our HR colleagues who help us co-manage the LinkedIn page, using it to share job openings [author's note: 320 global openings are posted on LinkedIn at this time] as content for the LinkedIn page, targeting the audience that possesses the right skills we are trying to reach. The social media team edits the HR material while our non-job posts focus on UNICEF priority issues and professional focused content."

…

"We are trying to push finding talent outside the regular UN pool, from the private sector, experts in a certain field, etc., which is a bigger priority than it was previously for our HR team. This is another major reason of our use of LinkedIn, as it is the #1 platform for the professional world."

Conversely, do you provide material for UNICEF staff to push through on their personal LinkedIn profiles?

"Yes, but not in an official or systematic way, though this is an area we'd like to improve on. We encourage staff to share stories and talk about their work for UNICEF on social media and to help them in this regard we have social media guidelines."

...

"After we relaunched the LinkedIn page, we held a governance exercise and discovered that there were three to four other UNICEF LinkedIn company profile pages, as well as individual UNICEF country pages. We brought everyone together into the relaunched company profile page."

...

"In addition to this we have extolled the virtues of our communications staff and any other UNICEF employees having LinkedIn personal profile pages as strategic platforms for themselves."

How do you communicate with your global offices? Do they share a server? Large organizations put a lot of great shareable material out on a shared drive or on the cloud, and all they need for access is the Internet.

"We share content with country officers, and they can share that content on their personal LinkedIn profiles, as well. We are creating a lot of social media packs, an average of one pack a week for the last five years on the various issues, priorities, and campaigns UNICEF works on: humanitarian emergencies, child protection, child survival, etc., on a digital asset management tool everyone in UNICEF has access to, called WeShare.unicef.org. This tool carries our photos and videos, as well as the social media packs, which are primarily communications resources for country offices, national fundraising committees, other UN agencies, and partner organizations. The press can use the media resources within those packs."

How nimble do you have to be to handle a new international catastrophe? Do some of your social media projects get pushed back when something else is prioritized?

"I would say about 50% of our social media content is on humanitarian emergencies. We have three social media editors, one focused on humanitarian crises, one on video content; and one on non-emergencies (development)."

...

"We have had quite a few protracted emergencies affecting children around the world for the last number of years — Syria, Yemen, Iraq, South Sudan, Central African Republic, the Rohingya crisis in Myanmar and Bangladesh — and we need to focus a good portion of our time on these emergencies. So being nimble is essential when crises are unfolding. UNICEF presence in 190 countries around the world helps us respond quickly to cover emergencies and UNICEF's response for children."

Using LinkedIn in particular, who are you trying to convince or cajole or signal in the public audience? Who is your "them"?

"For most of our social media channels, the audience is broad: the general public. But in the last three or so years, reaching millennials has become increasingly important for us, along with the global middle class. In social media channels, our primary focus is awareness-raising and advocacy. Around emergencies, we are asking for donations, as well."

...

"Our strategy on LinkedIn is slightly different; we are communicating in a different way, using different kinds of content to engage with a more qualified professional audience. Ultimately, we want to educate them about the same things but in different ways. But we want them to take the same actions as on other platforms, watch and share a video, make a donation, or answer a call to action around a crisis."

What do you want stakeholders and the rest of "them" to know better about UNICEF that you can optimize on LinkedIn?

"We have four big "cause framework" areas (other than emergencies, which are over-arching priorities).

The whole global organization comes together in communications, advocacy, and fundraising to support in these areas:

- early childhood development: the first 1,000 days of babies' lives, and the necessary care, food, play they need for proper brain development

- child survival: newborns up to 5 years old, helping them not die from preventable causes and ensuring they survive and thrive

- ending violence against children: including domestic violence, violence in schools, bullying, and online safety

- refugee and migrant children: protecting their rights when they are on the move in Africa, in Eastern and Western Europe, and when they reach the ultimate host country."

  ...

"In these four campaigns and in emergencies, we focus on educating our audiences and driving action. On LinkedIn specifically, our strategy is educating a professional, focused audience, those thinking about their career who might or might not be looking for a job, educating them on what it takes to work with UNICEF, telling the stories of UNICEF staff. We present the background of someone working in an emergency, in education, in donor relations, in corporate partnerships, and cover the skills, experience, and attributes are needed to work for UNICEF."

What's the best surprise UNICEF has seen that you can directly tie to LinkedIn?

"The fact that over the past couple of years, we have the fastest growth rate on LinkedIn, faster than on the other social media platforms. Without having to expend a huge amount of energy, our strategy has been solid, it ticks along nicely, and the growth has been very strong."

Thank Yous

First, thank you to Bill Brucker, Kristin Sinatra, and Hugh Reilly for their interviews and allowing me to feature their quotes in the book. I was very pleased to hear them speak of the same concepts and practices as I had advocated in the book. And, this was not planned!

Thanks to Regina Vorgang, for her outstanding graphic art and design work that made the cover and the inside artwork so pleasing to me.

Special thanks to Deirdre Silberstein, whom I have known and respected for the 17 years I have been a multipreneur, for her thoughtful editing, advice, and wise counsel to make this book a self-published reality.

And thanks to my wife, nonprofit clients, and consulting colleagues who provide me with the conversation, reading material, and intellectual curiosity to make the nonprofit sector just a little bit more business-like every day via my suite of secure electronic payment services and my dedication to servicing their social network needs on LinkedIn.

I will end as I started, once again thanking you for not only for reading this book, but for what you do. I hope I helped you achieve your nonprofit's goal faster.

Index

Bio
Marc W. Halpert

Marc W. Halpert is a self-described "multi-preneur."
Since leaving the corporate finance world in 2001,
Marc has started 3 companies, all of which he still
operates.

Two of those companies offer specialized, paper-
less electronic payment services to optimize cash flow
by speeding of payments, to:

- retailers, small- and medium-sized businesses (**Your Best Interest LLC**)
- nonprofit organizations, professional and
  membership groups (**e-giving**).

In 2010 he started his third company, **connect2collab-
orate**, to spread his LinkedIn and networking evan-
gelism to train and coach others. In all his LinkedIn
training and coaching, he offers professionals the opportunity to better explain their brand and position-
ing on their LinkedIn profile pages: who they really
are and why them vs. the competition.

- As a LinkedIn trainer, Marc has been recognized as a high-energy speaker at national and
  regional conferences and instructor to sales/
  marketing and HR/training departments at
  large and small professional service firms and
  businesses.

- He is one of a handful of nationwide "evange-lists" to train nonprofits to cultivate their talent pool, volunteer, board member and donor development opportunities.

- His specialty in customized personal coaching has helped individuals in all walks of life and industries to use LinkedIn to better achieve their professional goals.

Marc has authored numerous articles on innovations using the latest LinkedIn techniques for self-branding in national publications, both in paper and online. He serves as a subject matter expert for the business, technology and social media press. He has been heard frequently on WCBS Newsradio 880 AM giving LinkedIn advice on their business reports. He blogs every business day with a *LinkedIn Nugget*

https://connect2collaborate.wordpress.com/todays-linkedin-nugget/

His book for the American Bar Association titled "LinkedIn Marketing Techniques for Law and Professional Practices: Techniques that Excel," was published in June 2017.

This is his second book.

What Nonprofit Clients Say About My Work

My LinkedIn training techniques help nonprofits and membership organizations.

When an individual's LinkedIn profile tells *why* I do what I do, the organization looks even better to donors and other stakeholders.

My work is helping others:

- Association Executive Director: "You know your stuff thoroughly. Every attendee was so pleased."

- Nonprofit professional: "I've managed to incorporate many of your suggestions into my profile...I'm still working on it—always in process, as you said."

- Another nonprofit manager: "I wanted to thank you in person for delivering such an impactful presentation at a time when I needed it most."

- From the Director of Development at a nonprofit: "It is just amazing what can be done... We have been very happy with your service and appreciate all your efforts for us."

Made in United States
Orlando, FL
20 November 2022